A LIFETIME OF DYING

A Lifetime
Of Dying

ELIZABETH BARTLETT

HARRY CHAMBERS/PETERLOO POETS

First published in 1979
by Harry Chambers/Peterloo Poets
Treovis Farm Cottage, Upton Cross, Liskeard, Cornwall PL14 5BQ

© 1979 by Elizabeth Bartlett

All rights reserved. No part of this publication may be
reproduced, stored in a retrieval system, or transmitted, in any form
or by any means, electronic, mechanical, photocopying, recording,
or otherwise without the prior permission of the publisher.

ISBN 0 905291 16 6

Printed in Great Britain by
Latimer Trend & Company Ltd, Plymouth

ACKNOWLEDGEMENTS are due to the editors of the following journals and anthologies in whose pages some of these poems first appeared: *Departure, Modern Reading, New Poems* (P.E.N., 1954), *New Poetry 3* (Arts Council, 1977), *New Poetry 4* (Arts Council, 1978), *Outposts, Palantir, P.E.N. Broadsheet, Peterloo: Anthology 1, Phoenix* (ed. Norman Swallow), *Poetry Review, Poetry Quarterly, Poetry South East, Poetry Supplement* (Poetry Book Society, 1977), *Poems of The Medical World* (M.T.P. Press), *Samphire, The New Review, Tribune* and *Use Of English*.

'God Is Dead—Nietzsche' was broadcast on *Books, Plays, Poems* (BBC Radio 4).

The cover photograph of Gwen John's 'Young Woman Holding A Black Cat' is reproduced by kind permission of The Tate Gallery, London.

Harry Chambers/Peterloo Poets receives financial assistance from The Arts Council of Great Britain.

For Howard

Contents

	page
MOUTHS	9
WILL THE REAL WILLIAM MORRIS STAND UP?	10
MY FIVE GENTLEMEN	12
PAINTING OF A BEDROOM WITH CATS	13
RUMOURS OF WARS	14
BETTESHANGER	15
OLD MOVIES	16
FRONT PARLOUR	17
NEUROSIS	18
DESIGN	20
SOUTHOVER	21
THE CHILD IS CHARLOTTE	22
BIRTH	24
LOVING NEIGHBOUR	25
DAVID IN ROMA	26
NO RAIN ON CAMPUS	28
GOD IS DEAD—NIETZSCHE	29
LISSON GROVE	30
DISPOSING OF ASHES	31
CHARLOTTE MEW	32
THERE IS A DESERT HERE	33
A WRONG KIND OF LEVITATION	34
I AM THAT E	36
PSYCHIATRIC CLINIC	38
CORPUS CHRISTI	40
IAN, DEAD OF POLIO	42
IN MEMORY OF STEVE BIKO	44
FAREWELL GIBSON SQUARE	46
IMMUNISATION DAY	47
SAFE	48
THE VISITORS	50
SURGERY	52
QUAKER MEETING	54
DESDEMONA	55
THE OLD WORKHOUSE	56
POLLING STATION	58
W.E.A. COURSE	60
BIOGRAPHICAL NOTE	62
DEGREES	64

Biographical Details / Notes On A Lifetime Of Dying

Elizabeth Bartlett writes: 'I was born of working-class parents near the Kent coalfields in 1924. My father was an ex-sergeant in the army and my mother a house-parlourmaid. Educated at an elementary school, I won a scholarship to grammar school, only to be removed at the age of fifteen to work in a hypodermic needle factory. I started writing poetry at school and was first published at the age of nineteen. I have been writing and publishing ever since.

I cannot explain a life-long passion for this private art, and I have no academic background or qualifications of any kind. Neurosis and five years of psycho-analysis gave me greater insight, and the WEA filled in a few gaps in my education, but it seems to me that the terrible mechanism of using words and making patterns from anything and everything which came my way cannot really be explored.

I owe a great deal to editors who published my early work—Howard Sergeant, Muriel Spark, Alan Brownjohn, and the legendary Tambimuttu of *Poetry London* who set up a teenager in print. In the jargon of the medical world, where I have worked for the last ten years as a receptionist and secretary for a GP, and for the Home Care Service, I am addicted to the writing of poetry and there is no cure.

The poem "Biographical Note" (pp 62–3) will give more details. I am at present alive and well and living in Sussex.'

A Lifetime Of Dying is Elizabeth Bartlett's first full collection. The poems in it are not arranged in chronological order, but the span is from 'Design' (1942), written at the age of eighteen, to 'A Wrong Kind Of Levitation' (1979). The collection includes several poems which have appeared in recent *Arts Council* and *Poetry Book Society* anthologies.

Mouths

Mouths are pink tunnels for supermarket food,
For kissing in the dark, out of pity or fear.
A mouth tells us structuralism is all, the lips
Moving, destroying a decade or two in passing.

A mouth is greedy on one breast, an abscess
Forming on the other one. That was the same mouth,
Sucking for dear life, a book propped on his head,
His destiny as clear as a runnel of milky vomit.

How we mouth at each other, like goldfishes
In tanks, eating, kissing, talking, drooping,
Sucking. Sometimes no stiff words creep out
At all. Biting is forbidden. We are not cannibals.

Ah, but mouths can say such words
The heart lurches in its cage, can say words
So compelling there is nothing we would not do
To hear them just once more before we die.

Will The Real William Morris Stand Up?

People need contemporary poetry like a hole in the head.
They need freezers, certainly, and credit cards, mints
With a paralysing flavour, and half-baked bread.

The books they read are found in D.I.Y. shops,
Shaped like bibles and placed upon lecterns.
The wall-paper pages are turned with a correct reverence.
Debate goes on in these high rooms, hourly, daily.

Will the paper match the carpet? Will the carpet
Go with the curtains? It will cost much more
Than the pattern of words we painfully arrange
To paper up the cracks in ruined houses
Full of dripping taps and badly fitting doors.

The pastoral patterns catch the eye.
They will fit in with the stripped pine.
William Morris lives again in flowers not words.
Whoever would stretch out a hand to pluck
Us from the shelves? We should have such luck.

The library, which is next on the list
For Saturday shopping is well-used,
Make no mistake. The whodunnits and biographies
Slide along the glass counters like goods
On an assembly line or pre-packed foods.

Powerful and puny, we stand thin and sickly
Next to Plays. Sometimes the date stamp
Doesn't alter from one year to the next.
Thickly crowded we occupy a very small space.
There is no doubt we are undernourished,
Patently unread.

Publishers feed us spoonfuls of patronage,
Magazines allow us the bit the typographer can't use.
We turn hopefully to each other, only to find
The deaf can't hear the deaf, the blind
Can't lead the blind.

Yes, that's the one, the one with everlasting flowers
To decorate the walls which hold us, and wherein
We may lie down to make love and pass the hours
With all the thoughts that poets write about,
And make them ours.

My Five Gentlemen

Prostitutes have clients, wives have husbands,
Poets, you will understand, have editors.
A mediaeval saint had lice which quietly left him
As his body cooled, their sustenance removed from them.

I have my five gentlemen, one of whom really was
A gentle man, courteous and kind, his rejection slips
Even appeared to be some kind of acceptance,
His face never seen, his care meticulous and honest.

Two was firm and neatly pruned my lines
Like a competent gardener tidying an unwieldy tree.
Faced with mis-spelt, badly typed pages,
He was even provoked into swearing mildly at me.

Three was a witty man, who wrote letters
On a kind of elegant toilet paper, and seen
At a party looked as practised at his social life
As he was at his poetry, though thickening a little.

Four was a shocking surprise. He was not at all
Pretentious. Squinting furtively at him, silent and wary,
I saw this pleasant face, heard a quiet voice, and saw him
Lasting more than a decade or two, a rare animal.

Five is dead, of course. His failing health
Was a comfort to me, though not to him,
Naturally. His death removed one more market
For battered goods, and proved a welcome release.

Rest in peace, I thought (for I always think kindly
Of the gentlemen who direct me to the pages
I am to sit in). I can only hope to be re-cycled
And end up more useful than I would appear to be.

Painting Of A Bedroom With Cats

The curved cane chair has dented cushions, the cats
Catch spiders and craneflies on the wardrobe tops,
The guitar lies in its funereal case, the road is quiet,
The apple trees have dropped their fruit in the grass;
Lenin is alive and well and living in Brighton.

The pale watercolour of East Chiltington church
Is crooked on the wall, towels hang like limp flags
On the radiator, the typewriter lid is covered in dust,
The sunflowers are dying in the lime-green mug;
Virginia Woolf is alive and not well and living in Rodmell.

The map of Sussex lies like a large whale among the dolphins
And the coats of arms in a curly formal freckled ocean,
Manuscripts lie like abandoned testaments on the table top,
The bright bedspread is folded neatly at the foot of the bed;
Caxton is alive and well, and living in Bruges.

The fluff stirs under the bed, and the drunks come home,
Singing under the ash tree growing near the iron gate
Which never shuts properly, frail Michaelmas daisies
Glow faintly, a late rose blooms, tattered and mildewed;
Hitler is alive and well and living in Notting Hill.

There is a crack in the ceiling, like the life-line on a hand,
A green plant in a pot, but not a pot of basil,
Stands on the loosening tiles, warm empty clothes
Press against each other in the cupboard, like lovers;
Proust is alive and young and living in Combray.

Rain is coming in from the west, the garden is lush and damp,
The drought is over, and the day is at the eleventh hour,
Sleep is nearly here on fern-patterned pillow-cases,
Books slither to the floor, cats are stretched on the quilt;
Gwen John is painting a lifetime of dying in a room like this.

Rumours Of Wars

My father taught me the tactics of war.
He practised them daily with my mother.
She was always the defeated one, silenced
By his eloquence, his sergeant's ways.

My mother taught me the use of mute insolence,
The correct care of the daily battlefield,
Black-leading stoves, polishing lino and chairs,
Forbidding long hair or fancy clothes and shoes.

My grandmother taught me how to suffer.
'There will be wars and rumours of wars'
She quoted from her bible. I knew that
Already, waiting for skirmishes to start below.

My sister taught me the ammunition of words,
'Liar, pig, cheat, teacher's pet, tell-tale-tit'.
Inadvertently she showed me monthly wounds,
Careless with the concealment of dressings.

My brother taught me that I could commit
Atrocities, forcing him into a dark cupboard,
Telling him of people who pulled small boys
Through the iron gratings over basement windows.

My aunt taught me that great power to charm
And wheedle loving but childless women,
Milking them for money or for favours,
Adept as any politician at a peace treaty.

Soldier's children, we watched our father's
Uniform moulder away, his stories of India
Bored us to tears. Insubordinate kids we fought
To get out and look for encounters of our own.

Betteshanger

Little Wales beyond England would you call it?
Myfanwy called it the miners' end of town.
We were the pale-faced children of the sea;
They had fathers who mucky came to bath
At the end of a shift. We listened when the light-ship,
Mourning in fog, cried near the Goodwins; they knew
The klaxon call from the mines, accident by fall
Of coal or rush of water. We lay rigid in our
Separate beds, Anglo-Irish and Anglo-Welsh,
Studying Latin and the world of Hollywood,
Where never a miner or a fisherman died,
Just Ginger Rogers and Fred Astaire
Dancing on an endless flood-lit stairway,
Top-hat and tails, no coal in the outhouse,
Or fishscales on their thighs, or money
In tin boxes. Town and gown were never
So apart as we were on the grammar school
Train, uniformed with plaited hair.
Her father, with his blackened muscles
Held my dreams.
Did mine make her walk like the mermaid,
Treading on knives?

Old Movies

The cinema lights are dimmed, the curtains part,
old movies roll back our lives, and now
we sit in the ninepenny seats, eating sweets;
darkness is all around, *Exit only* shows, and *Toilet*
on the other side. The screen, enormous and sensual
reveals the well-groomed girls, the moustached men,
that broad American drawl, those two-tone shoes,
the trilby hats, and call me honey evr' time.

I thought Hollywood was Paradise enough,
for life as she is lived was certainly lived
there, moonlight on balustrades, and the long stare,
the unruffled hair, and the decorous embrace.
We cried a lot, taking our father's handkerchiefs
as Greta Garbo died so elegantly, untouched
by sweat or pain, managing those last few words
with hardly a break, dead in band-box condition,
her lover, neatly suited, distraught with grief
as we were too, hunched in the soft seats,
schoolgirls at a Saturday matinee, learning
about yearning, enrapt until the credits
rolled and we stumbled out, red-eyed
to walk to the bus stop and to home,

to a shared bedroom and a grandmother dying
of cancer in the next room, sweating
and in pain, and the gas-light lowering
as the meter's money ran out yet again.

Front Parlour

There is no way, I know, to see the waters again,
far far out, and a thousand steps to reach the sea.
There is no way back to the ditch he pushed me in
the first day of war, or to smell the musty
cottage he took me to when no bombs fell.
There is no way to hold the first books
in my hand—anti-vivisection, written by a dog,
who described the terrible room in which
he found himself, dog's Dachau, for humans
yet to come, but then, the brave collie
who rescued his friend from the straps
and the cage, and the men in white.
A Victorian shelf, there is not a way
of reconstructing it now, green chenille
curtains and a front parlour, glass vases
and a flecked mirror, and cold linoleum,
a table with brass-clawed feet
which I lay my hot cheek against.
There is no going back, only forward,
surrounded by things as unlike
that special room as I know how.
Why, if there is no way back,
do I hear the dogs howl, the curtains clash
on the brass pole, the sea
splash far out, and distant,
and the hard body pinning me down
in the September ditch,
as the sirens wailed.

Neurosis

I am a dark cypress driven in the wind,
And the quarrelling voices of children behind
The Sunday streets. I am the listener, waiting
In doorways for the sounds of struggle
And torment. I am the shock machine in the empty ward,
And the enemy soldier under the point of the sword.
I am a little boy crying out Dolore in his sleep,
And the dazed women in rusty black who weep
Outside provincial cemeteries, and a foetus taken piecemeal
From its mother, and an old woman dying
Of cancer in a back room. I am my own analyst lying
Dead in his bed with the marks of the syringe
Like a macabre tattoo on his white body.

In childhood I was the red lady of my own nightmares,
And the pursuing jeers, and the hostile stares.
I was Manuela dead in a German courtyard, and the open maw
Of the butcher boy's basket, and the threat of war.
I was the clinging Goodwins who sucked down the merry
Cricketers, and the drums at the tattoo, and the poisoned berry.
Did you see me lingering at the gates of Buchenwald,
Or running from Electra, or making friends with the bald
Syphilitic hawking laces on the sea-front?
I was all men collecting the dole in long lines
In bitter weather, and the accident siren shrieking from the mines.
You have heard my name called in the courts
Of law for perversion and murder, and malice aforethought.

Would you know me? I am also a young woman, growing
My flowers in season, feeding my cats, knowing
Little, but feeling everything, writing at all times
And in all places, working out rhythms and rhymes.
I make clothes for young children, a red kilt
Or a jacket for a newly-delivered child,
Assuaging my envy and covering my guilt.
Sometimes, from my husband's arms, I catch
A glimpse of the potency of love, like a mirage
Soon gone, and I wonder if I shall ever be whole,
Or always playing torturer and tortured in my double role.

Design

The blanched eyes of the aspens
Quiver at the field's edge, their mad cascades
Of butterflies turn swift and brittle,
A swirling precision of whites and jades,
Like notes in a sick brain, the beat
Of Ravel
Dying in a Parisian clinic,
Between white walls in a tree-lined street.

This summer field bears the weight
Of the brassy buttercups,
And the bodies of you and me
As we lie down together.
The field is as bright as the sands
Of Saintes-Marie-de-la-Mer,
Or the chair
Of the madman of Arles.

Southover

French rolls I bought, running
Velvet-slippered, humming
Bach, on cool October mornings
In the nineteenth year.

A marriage bed I found, dancing
A swift primeval dance
Between laundered sheets. Young
I was, and the tune difficult
To follow, many-melodied
Like Bach.

Calm walls I had, wooden floors
And painted windows watching
A leaf-strewn road; no trousseau
And a leaping-shadowed ceiling
At my consummation.

Crazy music I heard, cacophony
Of colour and breath, and spindleberries
In a pale grave jar,
A back cloth
To my strange triumphant silences.

A lover I had, clear voiced
And double-lived, like Bach.
He walked
About my rooms, an unexplained
Hypnotic walk; he touched
My breasts, and lit a fire
In my house,
And in me.

The Child Is Charlotte

Wish me out of this coma of fantasy
Into which I have fallen, and lie
Floating and submerged by turns,
Pacing the paths with Charlotte
In my arms. The die
Is cast against me, the burns
Wrinkle on my arms, the symbols
Of all that may make or mar a child,
And the child is Charlotte.

The drifting shawl severs the dead
Twigs in the dream's edge, the forceps
Fail, the blessings deceive us,
All is broken and lost in the oncoming
Dusk, in the oncoming head.
Who will receive us,
When we are separate,
After the pain has been ridden,
After the incubus returns unbidden?

I have so little to give you,
Only the tedious knot of pain,
No sooner unravelled than knotted again,
A faltering facility with words,
A mountain from my molehill's feeling.
A deft hand to spin your name
In the fall of a peeling.
No love, if my own love gutters and dies,
And the darkness rushes in.

Paltry the gifts for Charlotte, no magi
Travelling the interminable wastes
For a new-born child, only
Implacable genes, uncertain myrrh
For so long a season. The lonely
Gold is no reward for her,
Death being no solution for a wayward child,

Grown weary with waiting, grown wild
With anguish, and the child is Charlotte.

All we have for the moulded head
Unmeshed, is our own particular web
Of mingling and unformulated beliefs,
And the varying means by which we live,
The blunt fingers on a recorder,
The poetry written with difficulty
Between supper and sleep, a retinue
Of cats, to have and to keep, all
Their nine lives, many-covered books
Longed for, to suck and chew upon,
Being nearest to hand, but forbidden
Always.

Here is your bubble, my bountiful.
Here is your room.
Here to excrete and vomit and bloom
Like a rose.
Here is my womb
Clinically correct.
I hope you may never know
The reluctance
Of this blossoming turmoil.

Who do we think we are, to engender this life,
To set it stumbling forward, out into those passions
Of fear and mistaken ecstasy, down darkening years,
Reproachful, as we have been reproachful? Fashions
Change, wars divide and split the world,
Childhood is gone, the body buds and breaks,
Blooms, deteriorates, trembles, grows old,
Grows still, is bundled away, lies
In a coffin covered with sacking
On some remote railway platform.
Who are we to lie like gods on a cotton quilt,
Listening to the spread of rain through stem
And root and layer of soil, and from the dregs of guilt
And distaste bring forth this infant, this old woman,
This child called Charlotte.

Birth

When they gave you to me you were redolent
Of acrid badly-made soap and blood,
And indeed you were covered with a waxy layer,
Like rice-paper on a macaroon, or cottage cheese.
You had obviously done some very heavy laundry
In the womb, using soda, wringing your hands,
Purple and sodden like a washer-woman,
Whose feeble fingers have mandarin's nails
With which you scratched your face, adding
To the general air of wear and tear and age.
And yet you were so young, a few minutes,
And the placenta not yet flowering in the bowl,
Your doll's clothes still airing, your air-way
Choked with mucus. All night we drained
You like a boiled potato, tipping you up
And, newly-washed we looked upon your great
High forehead, and your thin crop of hair,
And marvelled that you had travelled so far
Through such a small tunnel, no cuts,
No stitches, no forceps, just a long journey
And a small body, like a fish, sliding neatly
Into a quiet house, and an old bed,
Where no other child had been born before.
You cried a little, and then, exhausted, fell
Into the deepest sleep there is, apart
From death, and I lay flat and empty
Awake all night, tired beyond sleep,
Fearing and hoping beyond all bounds
That you would not live to curse your birth
As many have done before you,
And will do again.

Loving Neighbour

This summer, the unfamiliar sea, and the driftwood
Leaning against the wall in the sun, and the pile
Of kindling grown too big, because the letter says work,
Because the letter says stoop and carry,
Drag the wood from the cargo ships a mile
Over the rocks, and you may miscarry.

The sea has deprived the happy pregnant women
Of their golden oranges. They rot in the sand
Among the broken crates and the twisted branches,
And the bloated life-belts under this sultry
Summer sky, but the letter says work, do not stand
And think, but work, and cancel out adultery.

These long weeks the sea has been too calm,
The sun too bright and regular to hold my pain.
Even the letter says storm and the waves beating,
For the letter says work, and the storm brings wood,
And flings it along the shore, bright paint and salt stain,
Pattern and chaos, and sodden food.

To-night, the bell-buoy out in the bay,
And the gulls' feet pattering on the tiles:
And the path to the sands trodden hard,
And the house swept clean, because I may not marry.
But the letter says get up, add to the pile
Of kindling, and you may miscarry.

I do not know why the gulls are silent,
There is no colour in the sea and the sands are empty and clean.
In my belly your storm advances,
But my mind is as calm as this strange sad summer has been.

Where is my loving neighbour? Who will help me to bed?
The sea is my loving neighbour, and the sand shifts under my head.
No-one gathers driftwood by moonlight,
But I have done what the letter said.

David In Roma

David in Roma, under the gilded tree,
Turns a pale face to me,
From a Christmas which has gone,
But is here always.
Photographed in Roma, forever forlorn,
Forever four years old, he
Looks out coldly, grown
Grave and remote, sitting alone
Hand upon knee, then, now,
Under the bough
Of his Christmas tree.

Now in the streets of Rome the children run,
Now in Regents Park the creak of hoop, the click of gun,
And the bleating doll cries ma-ma, spinning a cry
Between London and Rome, faster than his aeroplane can fly,
Cries ma-ma ma-ma under the frowning sky,
Between the naked trees, along the paths, here where no sun
Breaks through, and there, where the children run
With David in Roma.

Is the Spring early in Rome?
Tell me, does the dome
Of St. Peter's shine like the dome
Of St. Pauls?
For you, the morning walk
Must be taken somewhere; but not here,
And the games and the talk
Must be in one language or another,
Out in the street, out in the via,
At one time or another,
There or here.

No one walks in the park when the sour fog swirls.
This is no weather for boys and girls
To come out to play at birth and death; the child
Who dies on the green battlefields of St. Pancras, the child
With a baby for each lived year, like a mild
Victorian mama, feeling the china skull beneath the curls;
They are all at home till the grass is dry and the fog unfurls,
Like a day in Roma.

David in Roma, David in Rome,
David in London, David at home,
Over the mountain and over the sea,
The Pope can dance with my Lady Lee.
O-U-T spells out,
And out goes he.

No Rain On Campus

In the formal nineteenth century parkland
The University buildings rise like glass palaces;
The young men have long hair. They look like princes,
Or like Rossetti, whose vacant house I used to pass
On the Kent coast when I was a child on holiday.
They look careless and young, definite and vociferous—
No eight till six in a hypodermic needle factory
As I did when I was younger than I am now.
One pushes a pamphlet into my hand. *No rain on campus*
Is the curious slogan I read, duplicated on purple paper,
A crude drawing of a monster swallowing a child.
Solve your creche problems. Throw your children
To the animals. The monster has the look of a benign dinosaur
Made in the sixties with assorted plastic pieces
By a small child, not thinking he would join
The princes, the hem of his denim trousers
Dragging in the dust, and his hair flowing free
As a drowning maiden. *Picton is semi-divine*,
I read. Alas, poor Picton, who is he?
Hail Mary, mother of student, who am I,
Who dug no waste land on Margate sands,
Only a castle pocked with shells and deep with dungeons?
Like a mystical message I carry it with me,
Seeming for a while like the words of the man
Who walked with trousers rolled by the sea,
A young man in a dry month, waiting for rain,
But here, no rain, no rain, *no rain on campus*.

God Is Dead—Nietzsche

Daddy and I are always here, you know,
Whenever you want us.
We didn't like the things you said
The last time home.
Bourgeois, you said, and a word which sounded
Very like atrophied.
Daddy doesn't like the way you collect
Toilet graffiti,
God is dead—Nietzsche, and the reply,
Nietzsche is dead—God.

You can't expect Daddy to go round
With the plate in church
With thoughts like that in his head.
I worry too.
Structuralism sounds like a building-site,
Semiology sounds rather rude
In a medical kind of way.
The dogs are well, both almost human,
As we've often said
To you.

Please wear a vest, the days are getting
Colder. We hope you will not be so rude
The next time home.
Daddy and I have just re-done your room.
The blood on the wall hardly shows
After two coats of paint.
Cambridge must be very pretty just now.
I am, in spite of everything,
Your loving Mother.

Lisson Grove

After I left you, a thin vapour settled on my mind.
I walked past the rubber shops and the urinals.
I walked past the shop with the dusty 1910 shoes.
I walked past the crowding basements, the blinds
Were crookedly hung, the plants faded, broken,
The kids were yelling from first-floor windows,
All summer stunned and bleeding in Paradise,
In the vomit-stained rotting courts of Paradise.

After I left you, words would not hang upon feelings.
Grief, parting, good-bye, never. O God, O Lisson Grove.
I walked past the open door of the church, and incense
Was flung out at me like a rotten cabbage. Come,
Said the virgin and all the tatty saints, come, come.
Come, said the skin-and-bone Christ and his 7 foot cross,
But I walked past, dragging my own cross behind me,
Each step bruising my heels as it lurched behind me.

After you left me, the sun wavered and dimmed in the sky.
I saw a negress in a mauve cardigan picking her bad teeth.
I saw a grey lace curtain twitch as I sidled past.
I saw black hair-combings twined on a rusty railing,
A clot of blood blooming in the road like a peony,
And scrawled chalk genitals on a subway wall,
Like a message of primitive magic now lost to me,
And you, packed and gone and laid away, now lost to me.

After you left me, images obscene and sorrowful
Followed the jerking hearse of our un-natural love.
On a coffin of couches I lay down and wept for us,
And for the feet which walked in the 1910 shoes,
And the dolled-up virgin's swollen uterus,
And the mourning face behind the curtain,
And the hand which held the chalk, alone, in the dark,
And your hand which turned on the gas, alone in the dark.

Disposing Of Ashes

A gray day in June, as cold as charity,
The full-leaved trees sinister in heavy green,
The undertaker wearing his winter coat.
Our cold lies inside us like a cube of ice
Unmelting in the core of our being,
Untouched by succeeding summers,
For June will always be cold now,
However bright the sun, however fragmented
The light and shade, the over-blown rose,
The tall grasses seeding in a recession,
The tar bubbling on the hot road-ways.
Death stamps its mark on a month
And a year. Never will Jubilee tat
Be a joke any more. Sodden bunting
Hangs in the rain, swags and crowns
Disintegrate. Only the plastic flags
Survive, flapping disconsolately on fences
And front doors. It has been a wet week,
The street parties were a wash-out,
The public junketing an offence against
Private grief. Even Ditchling Beacon
Looks menacing, and the ashes not soft
As in imagination, but like pellets
Almost. We dump them among the rabbit
Droppings, and run through the mud
And drizzle, back to nothing
Where something was before,
Leaving our royal one soaking
Into the soft downland grass
Faceless to the sky.

Charlotte Mew

'When her death was reported in the local Marylebone newspaper, she was casually described as "Charlotte Mew, said to be a writer" '—from a memoir by Alida Munro.

Charlotte, to-day I walked along the streets where you died,
That remote and desolate Spring of nineteen twenty-eight,
With Anne dead, Ma gone, and the other two immured inside
Some asylum still, or dead, but lost to you, all hate
Shadowed and masked and laid away, whichever way it was.

Charlotte, to-day the balustraded houses balanced in pity
Above the chimes of sunlight and the waiting ambulances,
And all around, the soft and moulded web of your city
Hung like a shroud of sound, and the pigeons drank
From the gutters, nervously treading the sloping tiles.

Don't keep me. Let me go, you said,
And I thought of the first sessions
Starting in the clinics, and the bread
For the day's hunger in the ovens
Of the bakery, and the swirl of wings
Beating around the stained pillars
Of St. Marylebone church, and all the Springs
Which have restored to vogue or memory since then
Wavered and faded and dissolved until I saw you
As you went out alone and bought the disinfectant
Which killed you, Charlotte Mew, said to be a writer.

Don't keep me. Let me go, you said,
And you lay with your small dead
Face turned to the grey light
On the blank brick wall.

There Is A Desert Here

'I loved you in silence, without hope, jealous and afraid.' Pushkin.

There is a desert here I cannot travel,
There is sand I cannot tip from my shoes.
Over my left eyebrow is a greenish bruise.
There is you, and there is me. I cannot choose
But love you, though you wrong me,
And make angry love to me, a smack
Like a caress, a careless move, and a crack
Appears in your loving, widening, widening.
It was a bad bargain I made with you.
Your green eyes and your strutting maturity
Did not mix well with my long pale face
And my convent innocence, but they looked
At me, flashes of light, like sexual lightning,
Blackening my tree. At last I sprout
From the bole after all these years
When you might have thought my tears
Were gone, and my tortured tree was dead.

Come little creatures, walk on me,
Come little worms, slide upon me,
For no man ever will again.
I watched beetles and ladybirds
Long before you gathered birch twigs
To beat me in a field—in fun, of course,
And I will watch them again,
And grow old ungracefully, barefoot
And sluttish in my ways.
No more hauling of ashes,
I promise you.

A Wrong Kind Of Levitation

Trying out the kind of levitation he had suggested,
the Sussex fields lay variegated, rounded, diverse
as the marks on a tortoise-shell cat, a map like
an untidy chess board, the pawns capturing kings
and queens, the bright flocks of clouds pulling
at her hair. On to the mosaic of the Surrey hills
the cracked and crazy voices talked of lynchets,
bridle paths, foxes panting in their hidden earths,
the rain in a mizzle and a flurry stung her cheeks,
bloodless though they were, incorporeal, transparent,
down the alleys and tunnels of the freezing winds.

He had asked originally for various parts of her,
a small toe or an ear, a strand of straight hair.
Ethereal and tenuous, the wrong parts, tear filled
eyes, her hands like lizard's paws, tactile sensations,
entangled on the wooded slopes, lost somewhere in Kent,
somehow a wrong turning, somewhere a faulty diagram.
Stretched on her airy rack, she would not take
back the painful spasms, and killed by inches
severed herself, to re-assemble in a place
by a river, bruised but whole, quietly creeping
up the stairs to where he sat alone in his room.

It had all been a joke, he said, willing her breasts
like pale lighted globes at a children's party.
That was all he meant. It had all been for nothing,
that thermal riding where the owls called out at night,
and all the strident country noises, creak and squeak
and scream were like the howling of her separation.
Sitting crouched over other people's lives and lines,
and clearing a space among the papers and the books
he made a perfect jigsaw of her organic parts
and sent her home alone, kissing her lips as he
pressed them into position, opening the windows wide.

He worked alone each evening. Her clinging intensity
scared him stiff. Presented with this Brontë wraith
he regretted the sci-fi appearance of what had been
a harmless joke, to please his own need to feel
and touch, this mental and spiritual contact he was
always talking of. Her scattered witch-like ride
made him wonder what the hell he'd let himself in for,
sat her on his knee, vainly chafed her cold body,
and her thin white arms like ectoplasm at a seance,
which enfolded him too tightly for his comfort,
let her go with relief, reached for a glass and drank.

I Am That E

I don't appear on the pages
Very often now. At first,
Like a new toy, I was played with,
Seduced among the ferns, ravaged,
Defeated, and wildly praised.
I played the awkward role
Of step-mother to two fair-haired
Children, fair like their indiscreet
Mother. I wrote some poetry here
And there. Published here and there,
Mostly without payment or much reward.
Now, I see the country as your bride.
Among the budding groves, and trees
You are yourself, as your father was,
Watching the woods and fields, finding
Such infinite variety as no woman
Can provide.

This is the time of year, you write,
When little boys go away to school
And old men die, and wives give birth.
Your children, your father, your wives,
And one sad Austrian mistress
Whom you left for me,
You would barter them all
For a cloud or a tree.
We parted long ago, but still
We live together, and my dark-haired
Child walks by the river Cam,
With his head as full of words
As yours and mine, not knowing
A willow from an ash,
Or his father from me.

Now I appear as a figure, part house-keeper,
Part sexless menopausal creature, an interior
Person, surrounded by my urban garden,
Still afraid of the bleak downs and villages,
Cherishing my cats, lying in my mother's
Coffin, with her quiet voice and grave eyes,
Working where she might have lived,
Walking the bare brown corridors,
Surrounded by old people's trash and tittle,
Kissing their cheeks when I leave,
Like embracing a leper, I sometimes feel.
You are free to go far away into untouched places,
I go into imprisoned lives, imprisoned myself,
For I am that E.

Psychiatric Clinic

Wavering through the wind like the cry of a child
St. Marylebone strikes the hour on this mild
October morning.
Tchehov knew us. In mourning for our lives
We wait here on stiff upholstered chairs,
Behind this closed door marked adults;
But we are all children, though grey hairs
Disguise us and wedding rings adorn us,
Though children have been born to us
In our turn.
This is the turn of the year.
We have travelled here
Alone through the rain and the falling leaves.
We are patients, we are cases,
But we have managed our buttons
And tied our own laces.

Here we are.

A young woman inwardly crying
For a mother who will not come,
Who cannot come again, is gone, is dying,
In a second of time,
In the fall of a leaf

Here we are.

A blind boy holding his stick
Like a white gun,
Seeing a dead child stretched on the pavement,
Never seeing him
Get up and run.

Here we are.

A parson whose Father inhabits no heaven,
Creator of his own hell.
His church bells
Are the cries of his mother in childbed,
Twenty years ago.

Here we are.

A pale girl watching the rain,
Looking out through the bars of her cot,
Where the shadow falls
On the nursery walls
Again and again.

Here I am.
I wait here on my stiff upholstered chair,
With a rain-wet face and a dead leaf in my hair.
I am boy, girl, woman, parson; all pain
Is mine in the death of the year and the tears of rain.
Wish when you catch a falling leaf.
Where is the wish?
Only the grief remains.
Three flights up I must go, and many more
Than three flights back, before
I shall know.

Corpus Christi

This is the only decaying nineteenth-century house with a stable block
Left among the ranks of square boxes with small gardens covered with grass
And with central heating, a shower, a colour T.V., and two-car garage,
And a mortgage high enough to preclude the price of a literary evening class.

In the stable block, which lies well behind the stone pillared portico,
There is no heating, and a jagged hole in the faded flowered wallpaper.
Since some well-heeled family lived out their lives secluded in this house
Leading out their horses on to the uneven mossy bricks we pick our way across
Every Wednesday at eight, it was a receiving place for children in care,
And now a tarted-up Adult Education Centre with plastic chairs in the main hall.

Some places carry their past with them, and this place is one of those.
The tears that were shed the first lonely night here, seep slowly through
The old traditional ballads we are reading now, cruel mothers so far back
They were not read about but told and re-told, or chanted and sung,
The dead returning with the birch bark on their hats, the children returning
From some bed-sit in Wandsworth, or some grimy institutional hostel room.

Ballads are full of the babies born on the wrong side of the blanket,
As many of these must have been, led up these stairs, the unfamiliar name
Of stable block as incomprehensible as the kindly, over-worked staff
Who sent them to bed without a comforting packet of chips, or herded them
Out into the vast gardens to play and chant those rhymes which have such links
With the ballads we earnestly listen to on a faulty tape-recorder tonight,
The violent cryptic stories so like the horror comics the bold ones smuggled
In, not understanding Beatrix Potter, or Arthur Ransome with his special children.

These children were special too. Dead father. Sick mother. McCrimon ls gone,
Is gone, he will never come back, he will never come back, he is gone;
Quavering in Gaelic, the singer's cracked old voice uses her notes like a wail.
Corpus Christi I think I shall choose for next week's chilly session,
Feeling a wounde that is always bledyng as they lie upon their beds,
With comics under their pillowes and nits in their little heds.
Their hearts are surely turned to ston, Corpus Christi wretyn thereon.

Ian, Dead Of Polio

How old were you, Ian?
I was six and I lay
On a hot bed, hearing
The thin spidering shouts
Along the suburban roads,
Flying among the prunus
Trees, and dying behind
the front doors of Fairview,
The Haven, Guerison.

What were you like, Ian?
I was a fat child,
With fair hair,
And I would have become
A fat business man
In the city perhaps,
Or on the road,
Travelling in corsets,
Or natty kitchenware.

How did you die, Ian?
I died in a clean hospital,
Hot and tired and clamped
Into an iron box, like a beetle
In a matchbox. I saw
Mama when the tall
And turgid dreams burst
And fell about me,
And I was afraid.

Have you anything to say, Ian?
I want to say
That I was sick
And my head ached,
But it did not change
Into a toy on the bed,
Or a cup of milk spilt
On the sheet,
And a lightly boiled egg.

It changed into death
And delirium and spiralling
Dark, and a smiling gentleman
In black, and Mama gone.

This was an ordinary child who fled
From the semi-detached houses,
And television at five,
Who died, either in the sterile darkness of the ward,
At the age of six, or on the road to Leeds, cardboard
Boxes of corsets heaped on the worn back seat, at the age of sixty
Half in a ditch and smelling of whisky.

In Memory Of Steve Biko

Somehow the drains of feeling were blocked that week.
Biko died, and also a giraffe called Victor who was thought
To be mating at the time, and fell and couldn't get up again.
For Biko, also, it was a fall into death, the cause
Unknown, but guessed at, something far more disturbing
Than a very large animal, hauled to his feet, and perhaps
One day to be stuffed. We all know who hogged the news,
A simple but prolonged death, a pretty girl keeper,
Not a young black man.

We who mourned him were not the giraffe mourners,
And we measure with our eyes the space he died in,
And the means that brought his life to an end,
And the fact that good does not triumph over evil,
If indeed it ever did. Cradled in soft arms
With a girl's hair on his cheek he would never
Have believed his luck, but thought it one more
Trick in a diabolical game of cards.
Steve Biko, the sweet voice cries, lie here
Against this bale of straw. You were said
To have died on hunger strike
But this was not the case.

There will obviously be very little left
Of you to stuff as a memorial in King Williams Town,
And your mating days are over now
All your days are over now, for good and all.

As the news came in the following weeks
It seemed he died, as they say, under interrogation,
Said to have laughed at his keepers, said to have
Died of brain damage, naked and manacled.
He was careless enough to have injured himself,
Or so it would appear. The animal died
Like a man, the man like an animal,
As the drains of feeling gradually unblocked,
The canvas hoists were folded away,
The manacles were shown in the courts.
No one was to blame, was the verdict.

In two minutes flat.

Farewell Gibson Square

(*for Dr. Susan Heath*)

We did surgeries together. I warned her
Who liked litigation, and who were devious,
And who were mildly insane.
We managed to break a patient's arm
Between us, when he fell unconscious
To the floor. In the surgery,
I ask you, what shame. True the patient
Was deaf, and didn't hear our questions.
Compassion ended in gusts of laughter.
Not seemly. She wasn't a seemly girl,
Newly qualified, tat became her;
She wasn't sure if medicine
Was her thing. Lying in bed, smoking,
And reading, was. She taught me
How to pour a Guinness slowly;
She was pale and slow-spoken, witty
And thin.
Hospitals got her down, she said,
After a while, that is,
And furnished rooms made her puke,
But pubs and jumble sales
Were her natural habitat.
At last I heard she'd got a job
In a chest clinic, smoking illicitly
In the toilets, no doubt.
Fair Susan, with your Afro hair-style,
Your pot-plants, and your miniscule
Bank balance, I miss you.
Professional boredom has settled in
Again, and patients go home whole.

Immunisation Day

Some sit pale and scared, not touching the comics,
Waiting their turn, silent and tense. They are the ones
Who know about pain, but do not cry, frozen like rabbits
In their tracks. We, the predators, fill up syringes
Talking of jabs with the carelessness of a weekly chore.
Once in a while one child flies round the room, moth-like,
Screaming. We, the giants, grab him, hold him down,
And the wings fold, he is carried out, stuffed with sweets,
Sees us in his dreams at night, knocks against the trolley.
Last of all comes the survivor, who bares his own arm,
And when it's over says with distaste and severe honesty
'You hurt me. That bloody hurt, that did'. We recognize
The others, but he disconcerts us, and he kicks the door
As he goes out, leaving a mark like a scratch on white skin.

Safe

'*Incest is common in large families, both mother and daughter conniving in keeping the father satisfied, with payment as part of the deal.*' (Social worker's report.)

The father pays his dues. Once dandled on his knee
She now lies down to receive him obediently.
At first she cried, but thought the money easily won,
Dreamed of other things while he laboured above her,
His eyes seeing the likeness to her mother, the same
Hair, the same turning away. Enraged by this sometimes
He hit her. The mark faded by Monday, and the school
Was so large, a slight weal on a girl's cheek
Went unremarked.

The mother lies alone in the back bedroom, her fist
Clenched as she hears the same slap she once kissed
Away, but now tries to forget, shifting her heavy body,
Enduring her prolapsed womb, wiping her sweating face.
Sometimes when the social worker comes she betrays
Unease, drops a cup. Hot flushes multiply like weals
Upon her face. There is something in this house which
A trained mind senses, but silence is all she receives,
There is nothing untoward.

The daughter likes the week-days. All the lively boys
Who followed her out of the womb laugh and make a noise
In their communal room. She dreams of a sister
Who would have taken alternate weeks perhaps, sharing
The burden of his drunken body and her mother's
Pale secrecy. He penetrates her deeper than she knows,
For all her men and even her sons will have a look
Of him, and they will all complain how quiet she is,
Avoiding the neighbours.

The social worker writes out her notes, yawning her way
To bed. Leary B., navvy of Irish extraction. Leary J.
Menopausal, depressed; girl sixteen, six boys, overcrowding,
Reports on the Leary boys, wild, cheeky, smoking already,
Nicking cigarettes, out late, truanting from school.
Leary. Mary, a quiet girl in stylish clothes, with fine
Long hair, attends school regularly, stays at home
On Saturday nights. At least, she thinks, one child here
Is safe from harm.

The Visitors

'This patient was obviously hallucinating as I spoke to her.' (Consultant's note.)

There was one in the room, thinking of the sherry
he would have before lunch, rocking slightly in his chair.

There was another opposite him, grey hair falling
across a face like a coy but ravaged schoolgirl.

There were others present to whom she would have talked
had he not asked her tedious questions, eyeing her.

They were invisible to him, his ego balanced well,
his libido functioning perfectly, his accountant satisfied.

Sometimes their faces got between her and the desk,
mocking and bony, whispering foul insinuations.

When they advanced too far across the carpet
she wanted to get up and tell them to go away,

but his tight clinical voice held her poised
between the overt grins and the beckoning hands.

In the end, he won, and the others bobbed like balloons
in a corner, unmistakably there, but further away.

At last she was compelled to tell them to go away from her,
though she could see them reflected in his glasses, waiting.

He asked her questions, and noted down her hesitant answers
in a precise hand on a long yellow form.

In the end, he formally ushered her out into the corridor,
the faces, mouthing obscenities, followed in a muddled bunch,

crowding with her through the narrow door, escorting
her back to the ward where they settled in like squatters,

one on the end of the bed, some by the locker,
and one who laid his head on her pillow, talking softly

until she fell asleep abruptly, and for a while
the visitors crept away silently or floated gently out,

leaving only the faintest trace of their presence,
like a perfume or a discarded cigarette burning away.

Surgery

On my desk lies an informative leaflet about lassa fever,
And also a note on which is scrawled 'Can the doctor come.
Mum is poorly again, and oblige, yours truly. P.S.
Can't phone, box not working.' My phone rings,
And 'nocte', I write, 'two tabs, mare 1 tab, 10mg',
And answer the call at the same time. If I sound distant,
So does she—South Africa maybe, bleeding in Soweto,
But no, she has a sort of head-ache, and no, she cannot
Come this morning, because she's having her hair done.
Tonight perhaps, when the whole circus starts again,
The lion roars, the clown feigns dead, the tent
Shudders in the wind, the patients applaud.

The post is waiting to disgorge a message of hope
At last destroyed, an X-ray form with a fatal shadow,
Or N.A.D., those divine initials to say there's nothing wrong,
No abnormality detected. Before I have time to remember
The warm bed I left an hour ago, from a mystical erotic dream
I only half recall, the surgery begins in earnest.
Some cough, some limp, some sit and gaze, and one small child
Runs in and out, so plump of cheek, red of lip, blue of eye,
And full of energy, he removes the S-TI ticket
From my Caligari filing-cabinet. If he were taller
Would he snatch the A-BA with his neat questing squirrel paws
Indifferent to where he is? He might, but half way through
The morning and half way through the post, I tear up a few
Drug company ads. Maybe I've ditched a miracle drug, or
Another thalidomide. Who knows?

I have unpacked the vaccines and laid out the syringes,
And listed the house-calls, street by street, house by house,
When I see him standing at the door, gaunt and dignified,
Wearing a look of such suffering that even the squirrel
Runs to his mother and buries his face in her trousered lap.
He is a terminal case, and knows it, but he comes each week,
And for a moment, detachment deserts me. I want to cry,
Come here, my love, and I will save you. I will kiss and comfort
You, and bring you strawberries out of season, and wine
In a silver goblet, and deliver you from all pain and sorrow.
Come into the dream I left before I came this morning,
Briskly unlocking the door on another day, another surgery.

Quaker Meeting

There was this silence, of course, except for the bang of a door,
And a cat snoring, but the humans hardly breathed.
The meeting house was a triumph of simplicity. Pity the poor
Creatures who died here when it was the village slaughter house.

I had been reading Plath before I came. Her blinding fierce
Bright flame seared the bowed and greying heads,
And one frail student who seemed to pierce
The cocoon of their faith coughed and looked afraid.

Shit-scared, I thought, and out of the well of peace
The hooves of the doomed animals sounded in the street outside,
Their excrement and blood smeared on hide and fleece.
Perhaps I thought too long on the suffering lamb of God.

No way, I knew, could I join this plain and worthy band,
These middle-aged, middle-class chosen few,
Trickling through our violent society like slow, slow sand
In an ancient hour glass, grain by faltering grain.

O, how the sands of time ran out that day,
And when the words came, and the spirit moved, how banal,
How pathetic, how egotistical was the way
They used them, and I was offended at their indifference.

However convulsive the schism between the smiling face
Of Plath, like some Hollywood starlet, and the company she kept,
I tread her paths, but warily, avoiding the place
She finally found her deepest silence, her eternal bell-jar.

Then there was this friendly trooping out into the sunlight, of course,
And the cat stretched and yawned, and I felt ashamed
Because they could not remember where they were, or feel the force
Of the butcher's knife or think what brought them here so long ago.

Desdemona

Last year's grasses mat the path up to the door,
Nettles higher than a man spiral upwards,
Fireweed is spreading, brambles flick and claw.

The house is like the one shrunken person there,
Lying with a dangling rail to hoist her up,
Surrounded by uneaten plates of food, a rotting pear.

I ask her. I say 'What would you really like?'
'Nothing', she says, 'nothing'. There is nothing
Left, but an indwelling catheter. 'My heart, I strike

It and it hurts my hand', I mutter. She doesn't hear.
It wasn't clear if she understood I was there
At all, sometimes coming, sometimes gone. I appear

At different times in the day with my turning key,
Ask her how she is, let the dog out, spoon-feed
Mash into her mouth. I am not a person. I am not me.

Why does Othello pad up the path behind my back?
Why do I find Desdemona sleeping so fair
In a huddled ageing body, her beauty gone, her mouth slack?

I tidy the room, picking up a fallen handkerchief.
Iago's there. No, it's only the doctor on his round,
Oblivious of mistaken imagery, immune to love or grief.

The Old Workhouse

It's very cosy here. Some kind and misguided person
Has carefully made garish curtains with yellow roses
And put them up at the workhouse windows. Of course
We don't call it that now. This is our geriatric ward.
No, Maggie, you can't go home to-day, not ever
Maggie, not ever, but you don't know it yet.
Somewhere, in this frenzied pacing she knows this.
She knows the end, as dumb creatures know the smell
Of the abattoir, falling on their knees under the blow,
Ready for the well-kept tables of hotels and pensions,
Their flesh laid out on decorative plates, the wine
Blood red on the right hand, the waiters discreetly hovering.

It's at the back of beyond, the reluctant visitors say,
And she doesn't know me when I come, so what's the use.
She thinks I'm her sister Flo and when she wets
The polished floor she thinks it is the waters of the Usk
Where once she paddled as a child, the water
Cool and fresh, not warm and disgraceful. (Enter
An auxiliary downstage left with bucket and mop,
And disinfectant.) Everyone pretends it hasn't happened,
Except Maggie, who quietly weeps and asks again
To go home, away from this dreadful lunatic place
She doesn't remember being brought to, and from which
Dick would take her, if only he were alive.

Richard and Margaret they were then, somewhere about 1900.
She was a slender girl with a devoted young husband,
Who wanted her to have the best of everything, a car,
A house of their own, a joint on Sunday, a spin in the country.
When they retired they bought a bungalow in Sussex,
And no children sullied their well-kept rooms
For they never had either, only each other, and a Daimler.
One November day he died, stretched out on the kitchen floor.
The neighbours ran hurriedly across the neat front lawn,
Treading in mud which she carefully cleaned away
After the ambulance had gone and she'd phoned her friends,
Shocked that he'd left her to live out her life alone.

The country here is flat and ordinary, the trees
Seem aware that their purpose is to screen the old workhouse,
And not to grow in glory, as even the trees in municipal parks
Manage to do, sheltering lovers and children and old men
Still free to sit upon the benches in the sun and gossip.
This is not Dachau, don't be absurd. We do our best
To make the old folk happy, even if staff are a problem,
Coloured, and do not understand the language of the dying.
We prefer to call it their last home, and put them to bed
At six, well-drugged and out of the way, and quiet.
Hark how the Daimler's wheels hiss on the drive outside,
As Maggie goes forth like a queen, waving her last good-bye.

Polling Station

This park is a curious place,
Ravishing in the moonlight, the trees
Like iron scrolls against the Autumn sky.
Day reveals the dog turds crumbling
Into a fine dust, the graffiti on the walls
Of the cricket pavilion, the tennis courts
With wire as high as Buchenwald behind
Our backs.
This is our polling station for to-day.
The man I am telling with says that Spain
Is the place to go, the streets orderly;
The prisons full, I think, but do not say.
He went to the Costa Brava and ate his chips
With the rest of them. Our rosettes are different,
But we take the voters' numbers for knocking up.
I think I hear the knock on the door
In another country, another time, another climate.
I hear them screaming in the streets
Of Guernica, or marching sadly and wearily
Cloth-capped from Jarrow, my father's
Meetings in the front parlour, my mother's distaste
For the fag-ends afterwards.
There is no chance in this constituency for us,
There never was, and the polling station stands
On the right side of the park where the houses have names
And drives, instead of numbers and back alleys.
L'Étranger, I am always on the wrong side,
For the wrong reason, in the wrong place.
This park is a curious place. I am oddly comforted
By the boarded-up windows of the pavilion,
The empty Coke bottles rolling down the steps.
This is the place the aimless young frequent
On any other day, leaving their writing on the wall.
They do not come from the detached houses
Any more than I did. Inside this earnest
Provincial lady a young rebel cries to be released,

But she completes her list and then walks away
Across the park, back to Camus, unfinished,
Lying broken-backed at page two hundred,
Back to the cats lying entwined on the Spanish bedspread.
They would, of course, vote on both sides,
Always there for extra rations, never for extra work.
In the morning the battle is finished, the dogs take over,
The kids sprawl where the voters trod the day before.

W.E.A. Course

This evening we are doing Pasternak.
Last week we did Alexander Solzhenitsyn.
Outside this room which has wall to wall carpets
And stands illuminated in its own grounds,
The English autumn dies, modest and well-mannered,
The leaves swept away from the drive, the sun still warm
During the daylight hours, warmth reflected upon the face
Of our tutor, who could be my son, and looks like
D. H. Lawrence.
They should have warned me of Simochka
Who sits on my right in fashionable clothes,
And long blond hair, or Nerzhin,
Who was transferred at the end of chapter nine.
We sit in a circle, but Dante would not have recognized us
As persons with grave and tranquil eyes and great
Authority in our carriage and attitude.
This proves we have actually read The First Circle,
But this week I am glad to have travelled
The long train journey without Omar Sharif,
And seen the candles burn, and the iced rowanberries.
Across the room sits Lara, rather silent and also
A librarian, and next to her the Public Prosecutor.
Outside the wind is blowing, and the snow blocks out
This commuter town, silting against the door.
We are trapped, we cannot escape, we grovel
For a few potatoes, a few logs of wood.
Red specks and threads of blood gleam on the snow,
And the sound of gun-fire ends the class as we flee
In cars and on bicycles with our books under our arms.
Next week to Sicily with Lampedusa,
Nunc et in horna mortis nostrae. Amen,
And I shall be cast for the Leopard's wife,
Gesummaria, how far away the snow will seem.
It will be hot wherever we are, and Bendico
Will follow me home through the neon-lighted streets,
His dust will crumble and his smell pursue me,

As Komarovsky pursues me now, in his green car,
Dark as the forests at Varykino, cold as a Russian
Winter, in this Michelmas weather, cruel and ruthless
As the unseasonable revolution we are all waiting for,
With only a grammar of feeling to defend us.
Ah, Yury, the snow is falling, the stars have gone,
And I am alone; we are lost to each other forever.

Biographical Note

'I'm afraid I must ask you to compile a short biographical note. Where born, marriage, children, education, publications.'—Gavin Ewart.

Yes, I was born. I don't remember it too clearly,
But my mother did. She was there at the time,
A rag with a few drops of ether clapped over her mouth,
Another girl to disappoint my father,
Another mouth to feed in a terrace house in a colliery
Seaside town in the middle of the depression.

I think I was educated. Certainly I feared
The big boys' boots in the state school playground;
A scholarship and grammar school was another thing
Again. I learned to sound my aitches and to wear
Black stockings and a black felt hat.
I knew a bit of French, too, which impressed my Gran
Who had difficulty with English, let alone foreign tongues.

Yes, I was married. Two witnesses and a bunch of violets,
To a man not quite old enough to be my father,
Unless he was a randy teen-ager, which now I think of it,
Seems highly probable. A second wife, but not second-hand,
For he was that, I had to learn another set of tedious rules
About minor public schools, and not licking one's knife
After a well-laid three course meal.

Children. In the affirmative again. Say yes,
And you won't go far wrong. I inherited two
From his previous marriage. Clever kids they were,
At a progressive school. They managed a few back-handers.
There were ten years between me and the eldest one.
Once he punched me in the stomach, but he doesn't do that now,
Just verbally, once in a while, with deadly accuracy.

When they were grown my own child surprised me.
Gas and air and even pethidine in my own home.
Now the landlord's gone forever. I was taught to forget
About rent books and the dole queue, preparing my innocent
For the slaughter of boarding school, shopping
In Oxford Street for the right coloured tie.

No lovers, that's for sure, although you did not ask.
I was far too timid, and the deception would have killed me,
Supposed to be somewhere, when I was really somewhere else.
Cats I've really loved. Now, there's a thing, big-eared
Con men, with their dumb and devious ways. They don't write,
And if they are afraid they hide under the bed.
I'll join them any time.

Publications. One or two, or more. A baker's dozen,
Written in secret, published in error perhaps;
Always nearly making it, never really there.

Degrees

We are the ones with Fabergé's eggs
concealed about our persons, or walking
humpty-dumpty up the ante-natal clinic path.
No doubt you wish we were not here at all,
gazing out over the heads of sleeping children
at the boxes which are our homes, and gardens
full of prams and strung with washing lines.

We are the ones who don't appear too much,
the ones which modern English poetry
could do without. We don't hold degrees,
except perhaps of feeling, the mercury
shooting up and down like crazy.
Oh lord, the thermometers we break,
the sweaty sheets in which we lie awake!

We have no O levels, or A levels either.
We didn't fight and we didn't win,
we only ran to get the washing in.
Look out, you just missed us
as you crossed the crowded campus.
We were only there to clean the floors
and hand your morning coffee out.